TONES OF THE STELLAR

Kalu Onwuka

𝔊𝔓

Granada Publishing

Los Angeles, California

Tones of the Stellar

Library of Congress Cataloging-in-Publication data.

Tones of the Stellar/Kalu Onwuka

LCCN: 2013958170

ISBN: 978-0-9900203-2-5

ISBN: 0990020320

Printed in the United States

Dedication

I will like to dedicate this book, which is part of the *Poems in Faithfulness to the Divine* series, to all those who have shared the gifts of light and love with me either in formal or informal settings. You are too numerous to count but you have my heart-felt gratitude. I will also like to share the series with all those who love poetry and the everlasting beauty of simple words fitly spoken. Oftentimes in life, the will to act is not so much enabled in what is said but how it is said.

Acknowledgments

As always, I will first like to acknowledge Christ Jesus as the Lord of my life. He is my muse and it is his Spirit that enables me to write. Also, I will like to acknowledge that it is not possible to see through an undertaking such as *Poems in Faithfulness to the Divine* series without the loyal support of family, friends and well-wishers. You have all been there from the conception, writing and the publication process. I will like to acknowledge all your help for you continue to give me cause to hope for the best in humanity. It is such goodness that you share that evokes the pure love and good hope for better extolled within these poems.

CONTENTS

Dedication   iii

Acknowledgement   iv

Foreword   xii

Divine Thrust   1

Light precedes Rain   3

Vessels Well Fitted   5

In Resounding Thrust   7

Mastering the Way   9

Sweet Recreation   11

Place of Amazement   13

Able to Reach Heaven   15

Humility's Way   17

Sweet Spot Above   19

Statue Fit for the Cleft   21

Reborn in Light   23

The True Wealth   25

CONTENTS

Save the Future   27

The Earthen Spirit   29

Plea for Mercy   30

A Recycling Project   32

Glow of Hope   34

Bane of Humanity   36

Framed by Truth and Love   38

Light over Darkness   40

Kindness of Destiny   42

Closed Door   44

Share the Light   45

From Faith Mountain   47

Forever Divine   49

Creation's Hub   51

The Catharsis   53

The Soul or the World   55

CONTENTS

Days of Power 56

Lost Wings Found 58

Grand Picture 59

Misled into Dalmatia 62

Precluded from Divine's Feast 65

Except for Prayers 67

Golden Crown of Light 69

Kindness and Goodness 71

Sight in Light 73

The Wedge 75

Combatants in the Struggle 77

Eye in the Sky 79

Rare and Precious 81

In Ever Hopeful Love 83

Hand of Faithfulness 85

A Sad Tale 87

CONTENTS

Cross to Carry   88

Chiseled in Love   90

Common Thread   92

Reborn into Immortality   94

Strong Faith   96

Deep Nail Marks   98

Place of New Name   100

Power of the Anointing   102

The Citizen   104

Truth in Pictures   106

Family Portrait   108

Restored to Glory   110

Seeds within the Mountain   112

Love Reconnected   114

The Trailblazers   116

Age of the Perfect   118

CONTENTS

Redeemable in Man   120

Glory of the Cross   122

New Life Awaits   124

In Regenerative Splendor   126

Language of the Heart   128

Wellspring of Life   130

Of Healing and Restoration   132

Food for the Sublime   134

Good Flakes of Mercy   136

Spirit of Uncertainty   138

The Insatiable   140

Man of Good Faith   142

Child to Man   144

Embodiment of Truth   146

Branch of the Tree   148

Uncertain Bearings   150

CONTENTS

Lamp for Others   152

The Entombed   154

Scourge of Lust and Greed   155

Soul of the Divine   159

Womb of the Immaculate   161

Beware of the Storm   163

Teach the Young Well   166

Harbinger of the Greater   167

Drunk with Milk   169

True Cathedrals   171

Trap of the Enemy   172

Keeper of the Watch   175

Brother's Keeper   177

Breaking the Chains   179

Banded Together   181

Truth Speaks for Self   183

OTHER BOOKS BY KALU ONWUKA INCLUDE-

(Poetry)

Anthems in the Glorious Dawn

In Enchantment of Eternity

A Splendid Awakening

The Melody of Light

(Books for Spirit, Mind and Body)

Nuggets of Resurrection

Pulses of the Divine Heart

Etching for the Faithful Heart

No Hurry to Horeb

(Quotations and Insights)

Capsules of Divine Splendor

All titles are available as paperbacks or e-books and may be purchased through many retail outlets/distribution channels. All titles may also be purchased through Granada Publishers at **granadapublishing.com.** In addition, excerpts of the author's works can be read through his website at **kaluonwuka.com.**

Foreword

This book of poetry titled *Tones of the Stellar* is the third volume in the *Poems in Faithfulness to the Divine* series. The latter is a compilation of original poems that frames the author's spiritual as well as worldly experiences. It is a book of testimony that speaks about places that must be left behind in order to find much better in life.

There are eighty-eight original poems in this collection that are wide ranging in scope and tell compelling stories. The overarching theme is that all things can be known in the light of truth and that heaven has final approval in all of man's endeavors on earth. There is an underlying current that runs through the verses and pools them together in a way that makes for ease of reading. There are such poems that speak to the fact that there is a passageway to the divine, hope makes for a brilliant lamp, the cross is a bridge to new life, the better is forged in pain, the golden is found within God's mountain, a glorious life awaits the reborn in spirit and the divine loves the sharer.

The book makes for an interesting reading that the perceptive reader will find to be enriching and spiritually uplifting. It is sure to appeal not only to people of faith but to all those who still have doubts about the divine way.

Kalu Onwuka

Divine Thrust

Much can be transformed in a fleeting moment

By thunder and lightning borne of a common thrust

Incredible burst of energy it takes to lift the curtain

And rend heaven's veil for a glimpse into the hidden

It takes that dreaded by fearful and ignorant minds

By blind masses gripped in throes of uncertainty

To bring gift of enlightenment to those who seek

Such minds inspired by truth that aspire to know

The illumination received in the streak of lightning

Much like the inspiration that visits man in a flash

Is a potent sign in the heavens to tell the seeker

That all things can be known in the light of Truth

Divine Thrust (Cont'd)

Thunder and lightning may seem like dissimilar pairs

But are complementary twins from divine's breath

As hammer strikes the anvil and sparks fly to say

All things wrought on earth are first forged above

Lightning streaks to offer a heavenly perspective

In brief flashes to offer enlightenment in darkness

Tis torch needed to clear man's cluttered mindscape

A light given to induce vision and rekindle purpose

The flame of wisdom is a gift that can only dwell

In minds rid of fear and doubt that love the truth

In feet lighted to take timely and orderly steps

With outstretched hands that receive with thanks

End

Light precedes Rain

Man's cluttered landscape first needs to be cleared

So new life can have the needed room to emerge

Lightning is the torch well-suited to do the job best

Burns clutters of life so gardens of hope can grow

Nourishing rain does follow in lightning's aftermath

As showers for the famished that hungers for life

Rain is the enlivening stream that ceases not to give

For what it takes it returns in kind as duly needed

Rain makes it possible to be fruitful and multiply

In grace that gives to nourish earth and sustain life

Only by divine mercy does it alight or is withheld

At the day's end to rekindle life with smiling hope

End

Vessels Well Fitted

Been man's quest to do so and live to tell the tale

To capture lightning in a bottle and so be ever in light

For it the avails vision and insight to produce the new

To accomplish good designs and purposes on earth

Man that has the light is prepared for works of glory

As an immortal covered with cloth of the everlasting

He is a chosen vessel well- fitted for worthy service

An exalted one well-suited to travel in light's stream

The vessel of honor set aside for the Creator's use

Is a faithful one that believes and tarries to the end

Great tribulation and much toll it exacts from him

But such sacrifice it takes to fuel the light of love

Vessels Well-Fitted (Cont'd)

He who captures lightning is filled with divine essence

As a vessel immune from earth's troubles and death

Tis to have eternal life and peace that no one can rob

As vessel well fitted to mediate between God and men

End

In Resounding Thrust

Takes certainty of faith to live in obedience

To what God has spoken into a man's heart

For true faithfulness is about sacrificial love

That counts no hurts or cost for goodness

Man cannot help to be obedient to the divine

When his spirit is reborn in the light of truth

For his right and left hands are then dedicated

To carry out the heavenly mandates on earth

The right and left hands have preset roles

All ordained from the foundation of time

Roles that the hands clap together to reprise

To evoke thunder's resounding thrust in man

In Resounding Thrust (Cont'd)

One hand cannot evoke an awakening clap

Or serve divine's purpose without the other

It takes both of man's hands to clap together

To call forth that which tears mystery's veil

Voice of wisdom pleads with love's passion

Tells the left hand not to oppose the right

So love for Creator by creature can abound

And divine will become the order of the day

End

Mastering the Way

True vision and deeper understanding is for man
Who walks in the days of the second Sabbath
For he lives in the fullness of the kingdom of light
And is in faithful communion with the divine

The days of the first Sabbath are given for man
To learn obedience in the laws and ways of God
As first steps to reconciliation with the divine
In the long walk home through spiritual rebirth

The first Sabbath may be likened to infant days
As child learns language and ways of the parent
The attentive one who learns the language well
Will possess the key to decode his 'little' world

Mastering the Way (Cont'd)

Young that has been taught and mentored well

Is able to learn and fully understand his world

He will be in tune with all in his earthly plot

As the worthy whom the father can fully trust

Days of the first Sabbath give man the chance

To learn in the divining light of truth and love

The diligent one who learns in faithful obedience

Gets to walk in the days of the second Sabbath

End

Sweet Recreation

There is a field of delights that mortals dream about

Realm of the immortals that avails the fulfilling in life

Takes the greater enlightenment to glimpse that field

Where the gods who walk among men find recreation

Recreation of the immortals is for faithful hearts only

Whose souls have been washed and purified in truth

There in the freedom to be had in the field of dreams

Is the sweet recreation availed through love and light

Feld of dreams obscured to many is revealed to some

Only for noble spirits that are reborn in light to know

Tis the place of greater enlightenment well-reserved

For the certain of faith with love for divine wisdom

Sweet Recreation (Cont'd)

Regeneration is where the old is made new again

Resurrection is death of the old so better can emerge

The field of dreams unfolds as a divine playing field

For sweet recreation in regeneration or resurrection

End

Place of Amazement

Life in the greater enlightenment is for the man
Who lives right by God and by all his fellow men
He is one well-fitted on the right and the left
With both hands ready to join in Eternity's feast

Greater light leads man 'to a place of amazement
Into maze filled with hidden truths and mysteries
Where the answers to the bedeviling can be found
By the faithful who dutifully serve the divine urge

The doors are veiled save for the pure of heart
'to where freedom is for all but naught is for free
To receive the good and fulfilling availed by Love
The precious gifts in life not availed in lesser light

Place of Amazement (Cont'd)

The precious gifts are there in a divine showcase

With eternal life as affirmation for work well-done

Tis portion for glorious service in truth and love

For the sojourner who has made the Father proud

Man knows and is known in place of amazement

Tis where he that is of a low degree in the world

Comes at last to be exalted in divine measure

And to be 'trusted with things truly precious in life

Tis a place of honor saved for the chosen faithful

Real for all who are in communion with the divine

Who believe and heed the words of the Creator

But remains a mystery for souls lost in the world

End

Able to Reach Heaven

Sons of Providence; Daughters of Zion

Are all connected as offspring of Light

Into the realm of infinite possibilities

The limitless which never stops giving

Beyond the horizon into timelessness

To become transformed into the being

With spirit of the eagle in body of man

Befits the man for all seasons and ages

The faithful well-fitted is the righteous

A man with a spirit that'll abide forever

For he has become the golden-hearted

In the trusting love of the divine Father

Able to Reach Heaven (Cont'd)

He is one who has received the precious

For faith has rewarded him with the way

Taken away at Babel a long time ago

The means to reach Heaven from earth

End

Humility's Way

An impending doom looms not too far

As a comb now sorts through humanity

Tis hand of God that holds sway there

Knows who to keep and what to discard

To live in fullness of light is the reprieve

Calls for love of truth and sincere belief

For life governed by the words of truth

Will find refuge and escape into new life

There's a ladder that leads into freedom

From darkness below into light above

Tis same escape lifted Jacob into Israel

Leads from the earthly to the heavenly

Humility's Way (Cont'd)

Not by the works of the flesh or mind

But in the spirit of love through light

Given to those who yield to divine's will

And seek after God in sincere humility

Humility's passage is that rare gift of life

That is seen with eyes of faith not sight

The precious received by grace thru faith

Is for him who walks in true light to find

End

Sweet Spot Above

A special place where noble spirits dwell

Is spiritual realm that's far above the world

Place for men and angels to be neighbors

Where mortals become privy to divine's will

Top of God's mountain; Heaven's tableland

Is the place for the chosen to find true rest

Just like the communication satellites above

In a sweet spot between heaven and earth

By trusting God the faithful do come to find

Sense of true self and their place in creation

Where all's in harmony and there is nothing

To perturb the universal order and scheme

Sweet Spot Above (Cont'd)

Sweet spot above is the place of the sacred

Where the veiled and eternal are to be known

Measured words of truth from beyond man

There to be entrusted to only noble souls

Man becomes means by which divine wisdom

Priceless and precious may be shared by all

Not for the profane to use for selfish ends

But for the worthy to use for mankind's aid

End

Statue Fit for the Cleft

Season comes when the ascendant in spirit

Foregoes much in life in order to 'become'

Tis the call-up to the eternal and enduring

Time appointed to know and to be known

Many are called and appointed for 'fasting'

For those who desire and aspire for truth

Out of volition and the love for the divine

In fining season when faith separates men

Tis for anointing and christening in full light

So child of faith can become a man of God

To find wisdom's doors always open to him

And be able to find true fulfillment at last

Statue Fit for the Cleft (Cont'd)

Then is a statute to prove manhood revealed

To sculpt him into a man certain before God

A statue fitted for a cleft in the Rock of Ages

Who can be of effectual use in night or day

Tis the affirmation for full spiritual maturity

When man can stand upright under mercy

In season when all that is promised in faith

Is available for son of light to have thru love

The man worthy to stand in honor before God

Has to be pure of heart and without guile

For therein much has been ordained for man

In fullness of light shone only by the divine

End

Reborn in Light

Man who understands the power in sacrificial love

Is called to let go of the un-needed things in life

To step away from the lot which encumbers him

As the reasonable service for rebirth in divine light

Rebirth into new life is for the creature of hope

Led from famine and dearth to contentment within

In a world filled to brim with the nonredeemable

Where many are fed much but lack in substance

The reborn is a vehicle ordained to help men see

And is the depository for the needful things in life

One chosen to play a significant part in life's drama

Who fulfills roles and exercises power thru prayer

Reborn in Light (Cont'd)

His fervent prayers for divine help work wonders

To help stem the tide of evil that besieges humanity

For man reborn in light is embodiment of the golden

And a seedling prepared to be staple of the future

End

The True Wealth

The events glimpsed from behind the curtain of time

Are sprinklings of golden dust showered from above

As the rare and priceless to be safeguarded at all costs

For therein is essence of the everlasting and enduring

The precious which the faithful seek populate Heaven

As the substance of life and power that makes old new

All by divine knowledge and wisdom revealed to man

For the purpose of redemption and rebirth in spirit

The faithful pilgrim suffers temporary loss in the world

To become the noble in spirit laden with much wealth

Such that is availed is not the kind found in the world

But the needful and fulfilling that brings peace to man

The True Wealth (Cont'd)

The man that serves in the way that true love demands

Where one life is laid down so that many will abound

His offspring will bathe in the blessings of the Creator

For the promises and blossoms of love belong to them

Such a householder who serves in faith and compassion

Has a tabernacle to enlarge and greater flock to receive

He'll be bestowed with much as reward for faithfulness

Good gifts that neither thieves nor robbers can touch

Man's true wealth is children both natural and spiritual

God fearing fruits borne of the tree of righteousness

As the means to measure humanity's bloom or blight

To crown life's work and uphold man in his old age

End

Save the Future

Man's determined foe aims for the atrophy

For the spiritual strangulation of his offspring

The prince of darkness is a liar and destroyer

Whose sole purpose is to mislead one and all

Into the bankruptcy of soul that demands

Honor for the creature rather than Creator

He that sacrifices the young for material gain

Will stop at nothing in the crave for praise

For the spiller of innocent blood has no limits

Has no shame and never shows any remorse

In trading the promise of a fulfilling future

For the limited short-comings of the present

Save the Future (Cont'd)

The one bent on destruction of man's future

Seeks to defile the fruit of the righteous tree

To corrupt seeds of the young sown in hope

And entice with tools of the worldly as bait

All to beguile the unwary soul into the earthen

And put man's future at risk of spiritual death

But he that sees in the light lives to save babies

Saves as he models the way of truth and love

In sacrifices made so the young can know truth

Such know that the baby saved is good promise

As little that grows to be part of divine's edifice

From seed of hope to a righteous tree in time

End

The Earthen Spirit

The earthen realm entraps man like miry clay

To bind the unwary souls who tread therein

In consuming convulsions of envy and strife

With headaches and heartaches to attend

There's never peace or joy with the earthen

For life therein is all about living tit for tat

In torments, torrents and upheavals galore

That never produces or sustains the stable

Good can never come out of hell's hole

Only the unpleasant and the regrettable do

Tis that place of bitter and woeful endings

A womb of darkness and nursery of the ugly

End

Plea for Mercy

The way of light affords man the better choice

As passage way of humility to lead to the exalted

Tis an upward way for man to escape the earthen

And to have good fruits of peace and the eternal

Most of humanity have rejected the way of light

But chosen the downward thrust into the earthen

Where a gloomy doom and traumatic end awaits

In future needlessly sacrificed for lusts and wants

The world's not meant to be man's final destination

Only a spaceport for those with the passport of Life

A launch-pad from where the noble in spirit ascend

To an exalted and better home in heavenly places

Plea for Mercy (Cont'd)

Man will always be like a worm that crawls in dust

And never make the get-away to his home above

As long as he is determined to seek by his flesh

For passage from earth to heaven is found in spirit

Tis pointless for man to wrestle with the divine

For he can never ascend by his wits and own terms

He'll scheme as Jacob and never 'see' in that way

For only by plea for mercy will Israel seek and find

End

A Recycling Project

There's life in the kingdom of God availed to some

Many know not that life and have missed the Truth

Such are those that seek to sit pretty on earth

Men at great risk of condemnation and damnation

Such often seek and find fool's gold to heart's fill

Blind men who cannot see that the earth is a dump

Constantly being recycled by a non-wasting mind

Who searches with due care to save the redeemable

Sooner or later the point of no return is reached

When the good are salvaged and the job is done

Nothing worth redeeming left but pure garbage

Trash to be burned so the pristine can duly emerge

A Recycling Project (Cont'd)

The regeneration of the earth in order of heaven

Begins with the faithful redeemed for the new life

Such are the founding seedlings for the advent age

Worthy ones recycled into an everlasting kingdom

End

Glow of Hope

Bread for the eater from seeds sown in faith

Is good nourishment to afford man the rare

For the faithful ones who have been chosen

In way of truth and love that crowns thru light

Thru such many have come 'to the knowledge

Of the divine way and new life assured in peace

And escaped from entrapment by the earthen

To find sheltered life in the starry and heavenly

Wisdom's offspring have found their places

Among the congregation of enlightened ones

To be covered with essence of the everlasting

That yields enduring and fulfilling fruits in life

Glow of Hope (Cont'd)

Assurance and hope found through the divine

Shows in glow that shines out of the starry spirit

Tis light borne of the anointing of God in man

As 'sun of the righteous' arisen in many a heart

End

Bane of Humanity

Bane of humanity is enmity tween fathers and sons

To forestall enlightenment and blight man's future

But reconciliation is ordained thru the light of truth

To save the young from destruction's deadly grip

Man reborn in light is bridge 'tween the old and new

A pass-over to lead man from the lowly to the higher

With illumination of the divine and offering of hope

So that the estranged can be rejoined in spirit of love

The faithful messenger is he that shields the young

One to sharpen minds and renew ebbing strengths

Such spares many from judgment and condemnation

From drowning in the pool of the world's malaise

Bane of Humanity (Cont'd)

Serves hope well when humanity's seed is shielded

With God's truth declared and brotherly love shown

Gives the children hope and teaches the way of Life

To help trusting souls see in a better and purer light

The bane of humanity's the curse seeded from below

Works to keep men's souls entrapped in the earthen

But the power that sets free is passed from above

To re-establish the bond between fathers and sons

End

Framed by Truth and Love

Nothing can help man's vision better

Than power of truth and warmth of love

For truth that has been framed by love

Does become a mirror to bare all things

One that looks in mirror of truth and love

Sees the true image of himself therein

Will perceive where he has gone astray

And all that he is doing wrong in his life

Tis good for man to know what ails him

For he'll find healing by that knowledge

For the father communes in spirit with all

Who embrace the truth and fear not light

Framed by Truth and Love (Cont'd)

But God's spirit is offended by the proud

Who look not in mirror of truth and love

Divine power soon vacates from there

For the heavenly has no place for such

End

Light over Darkness

The reborn spirit is awake day and night

Ready to fight in the battle for goodness

But the flesh is unruly and inhibits that work

Unless out of the way when man is asleep

Evil flourishes under the cloak of darkness

Then do messengers of light raise up arms

With the Spirit of love in answer to prayers

To loosen the stranglehold of death over life

The ugly cords that bind the hearts of men

Are untied at night when man faces himself

Tis when darkness is exposed by light of truth

To vacate hearts where it had been at home

Light over Darkness (Cont'd)

The Creator remains unseen with man's eyes

But is reflected in the messengers of light

Prepared in love to serve his will on earth

As bulwarks to fight and counter all evil works

In the light that takes evil captive in its gaze

Reigns the imperative to overcome darkness

To dislodge seeds of fears and doubt in man

And awaken new life from the spirit bound

End

Kindness of Destiny

The messenger of light is that Holy Cow

Reared to maturity in a divine barnyard

The sacred who exists not for the flesh

But for meat of the spirit borne in mercy

The matured in spirit is a soul at peace

Who's merged into unity with the Divine

To escape death and become timeless

As a universal spirit to live for all ages

The heavenly father's lot is his business

And the kindness of destiny his blessing

For him who let go of fame and fortune

Saw those impostors for what they are

Kindness of Destiny (Cont'd)

Fame and fortune are rewards at best

To be blessed is far better and timeless

Blessings do not come with misgivings

But are good everywhere and anytime

Eternal life under goodness and mercy

Tis the package that includes all things

Then is nothing left for man to long for

When the heart's desire is ever fulfilled

End

Closed Door

Faithless life lacks moderation and balanced purpose

But is governed by an inordinate focus on the worldly

Such is a great trap when man desires to seek after God

As hunger for the material inhibits man's spiritual vision

The lust for world's materials leads to a spiritual demise

Results in a rejection and neglect of God's offer of love

For the divine and world's ways are at cross-currents

With choice of one or the other for all men to make

Tis the heart's desires and intentions that make the call

To order the wrong or right path that men take in life

Divine's way is a long-term choice and serves man best

For wrong path chosen closes eternity's door forever

End

Share the Light

Man who desires truth will find God's light

There to be embraced as the guide of his life

For tis beginning of wisdom to honor truth

As true understanding attends all who do

Truth regards not position or outside of man

Only the inside and conduct of spirit within

Gives man insight to live under divine love

And equips him for living in fullness of light

The Divine makes accommodation for all

To redeem the ignorant without knowledge

Induces the faithful man who has the light

To share same with others in truth and love

Share the Light (Cont'd)

The divine gift of spiritual enlightenment

Is from the Father to all willing to embrace

Tis availed freely for the worthy to have

So that true love can flourish among men

Many have been in darkness for too long

And lack spiritual sight due to faithlessness

Such are governed by the dictates of world

All dead men walking who know it not yet

Sadly they have been beguiled and misled

In little steps from the shadowy to darkness

Into hopelessness that foreshadows death

Where the glimmer of hope's much dimmed

End

From Faith Mountain

The faithful never gets more than he can handle

For the trials that he encounters serve to showcase

Measures of what God avails man through faith

And afford him tools for access to the divine vaults

Man must aspire to reach for the higher and purer

Where the beacon of Hope does brighter over time

So he'll be able to mine the limitless and bottomless

For the greater becomes available in a better light

Temptations get more challenging along the way

As the man of faith ascends up the heavenly way

But with Holy Ghost to tell and the Spirit to enable

A template for divine glory is ever available to him

From Faith Mountain (Cont'd)

The glory of the divine shrouds and enshrines him

As man reaches out to embrace the light of truth

The seeker after truth is soon merged with the pure

In faithfulness well-attended by goodness and mercy

There's always the refreshing when the spirit ascends

To receive Heaven's gift in light and to share in love

For the Father's promise is never to leave or forsake

But to bless the man who lives in goodness for all

End

Forever Divine

When truth and light lead man

Into the love that never gives up

Life is glorified beyond measure

So that death's grip is loosened

True glory belongs to the Creator

And things do become glorified

When God plays a decisive role

In the earthly endeavors of man

Eternity becomes the destination

When man's footstep is after God

He'll come into realm of delights

To join the everlasting song of joy

Forever Divine (Cont'd)

Eternity is for the forever divine

For man of faith deemed worthy

To receive the precious gift of Life

And cease from the fear of death

Death's no longer an end dreaded

But the start of a great journey

As continuation in a forever-land

Of a glorious life in new awakening

End

Creation's Hub

The sons are all woven from the fabric of life

Such are Hope's spawn reborn in light of truth

From the golden threads that are spun in love

With keys that make life's victories possible

The reborn have due reverence for the sacred

As custodians of truth who keep its mysteries

Such are deeply steeped in the purifying dew

That is distilled from the ageless mist of time

The collective memory of truths told afore

Unfold as visions in vistas that are eternal

To yield the precious to be treasured in hearts

And the priceless truths to be scribed in minds

Creation's Hub (Cont'd)

To the reborn in light is such true wealth given

As the beacons of hope who embody the divine

And congregate around the hub of creation

To seed the impulses that make for new life

End

The Catharsis

Passion that is such a heavy tribulation for man's flesh

Is good for spiritual transformation and transcendence

Tis the process that the faithful has to pass thru in life

So he can shed the weight of the earthy and worldly

Not much is needed on the journey of transformation

For many are the tentacles that tether man's spirit

Takes sacrifice to tone the muscles and be free of such

So the un-encumbered with strong faith can emerge

The passion endured for rebirth is a necessary means

Tis the catharsis which purifies man from inside out

And the door through which all the faithful must pass

To come home at last 'to the arms of the loving Father

The Catharsis (Cont'd)

The pain that faith exacts does serve a great purpose

It pares man's flesh so his spirit can join the everlasting

For it takes that which burdens the soul so heavily

To prepare and confer mortal souls with immortality

End

The Soul or the World

Man must cast away and bury his old nature in dust

To escape the beguiling allure of the impermanent

For the ego of the old man has an insatiable hunger

And an unbridled lust for the mascara of world's glory

Essence of the glory of the world is nothing but dust

As the wisdom of Solomon counsels all men to heed

Tis a bed of pride and self-glory for the serpentine

To blind man's spiritual eye and deny the clementine

Man cannot build on that which is soon scattered

By the unforgiving wind of time that erases much

Annals of history are replete with tales of misgivings

Pointless for man to gain the world but lose his soul

End

Days of Power

Days of the power of God are the moments in time
That are heavenly ordained for the works of glory
When there is much power for the faithful to use
And do the wondrous that's marvelous before men

The just and faithful God is no respecter of persons
And will do the same for all the righteous of heart
In abiding love that is everlasting and changes not
For those who aspire for nothing but goodness

The Spirit of the father is the motivating impulse
That moves man to act in faith on certain days
Such are days of the power of God that come about
When space, time and divine find common purpose

Days of Power (Cont'd)

Such times are the golden moments for the faithful

Whose wings of faith have come to full maturity

To receive divine gifts when stretched out in hope

For then are his prayers easily borne aloft to heaven

End

Lost Wings Found

Man loses his spiritual wings upon exit from the womb

Loses it as he views the world with the eyes of the flesh

He's soon left as time passes with nothing but the ego

As a spiritually moribund entity that craves earth's dust

The man of flesh can be transformed in the light of truth

So a new self emerges after due spiritual transformation

Reborn to rediscover his wings and to use them to soar

As a higher breed to alternate 'tween heaven and earth

The reborn is no longer a mud crawler bound to earth

But a gentleman whose mind is able to touch heaven

And rub off as desired from the lamp of divine genius

So an earthling can begin to see in light of the heaven

End

Grand Picture

The heavenly father is a God of purpose

Who knows the best for all in creation

A definite purpose and order is in place

Whether seen as good or bad by man

Creator does not want, haste or waste

For he has all figured and need not hurry

As he guides the faithful with patience

Into the foreknown and fore-planned

As the present age comes to its end

Runs out of appointed time and course

Some are able to read heaven's calendar

And keep appointments with the divine

Grand Picture (Cont'd)

The workings of the hand of the Creator

Coalesce in time into a grand picture

So that he that can perceive the truth

No longer casts in misguided pursuits

The life dictated by the heavenly picture

Becomes purpose driven and directed

To be attended by a spirit much at ease

With peace that cannot be disturbed

Tis at the juncture of time and faith

With man at peace with divine accord

That the greater vision dawns for him

And the mortal can join the immortal

The Grand Picture (Cont'd)

Man that has the shutter of the lens

Of the spirit within him open to true light

Thru faith and hope can glimpse so much

From the past all the way into the future

In images akin to time lapse photographs

The mind is able to view and to process

Significant trends and events of the times

As a creature able to read Creator's mind

End

Misled into Dalmatia

The man that has come into God's peace

Is surrounded by an aura of hopeful glow

But the faithless shine not from within

For lack of oil within the heart's lamp

The lens of the inner eyes of the spirit

Is always shuttered for the faithless man

For the souls without faith have their fate

Tied to that of this evil and dark world

Tis man's unceasing wants and desires

That abort the divine plans for mankind

To shroud him in a dimness of the soul

And to keep him searching but clueless

Misled into Dalmatia (Cont'd)

The worldly is flush with lustful attractions

To lead the faithless man into Dalmatia

Where his spiritual core is compromised

And the glow of the man within is dimmed

The man that is Dalmatian has dark spots

For spirit within him is mixed in darkness

He's not been soaked in the dew of truth

But blighted with the mildew of mistruths

He rejects the inerrant words of truth

And chooses to suit up with earthly rags

Rather than to allow God to cover him

With the precious garment of eternity

Misled into Dalmatia (Cont'd)

Tis wiser to love God more the world less

Thru truth that frees the earth-bound spirit

And washes the mud off the blighted soul

To do much wonder when truly embraced

The untruthful man obeys not as he should

Will not offer his best to God as he can

Nor live in love with all as he ought to

And is never fully blessed as he should be

End

Precluded from Divine's Feast

Humanity has entered a season of reality check

As the cosmic clock speeds to the marked hour

A separation of the wheat from the chaff awaits

To affirm the numbered worthy of redemption

The chosen are meat of the grain of humanity

Uplifted in spirit into a higher and exalted realm

While the rest flounder below in world's darkness

Men feted by the world but rejected by heaven

Such took God for naught and failed to do right

Lived for self and took other men for chattel

But others believed and trusted words of truth

And have come 'to fulfillment of love's promises

Precluded from Divine's feast (Cont'd)

The faithless who took the broad and quick way

Lived for short cuts and quick returns of the easy

Who used men for gain and forestalled the rain

Same are precluded from the feast of the divine

End

Except for Prayers

The Father makes much available

To the faithful filled with his Spirit

Who sow seeds of mercy on earth

And make the changes duly needed

Across the landscape of humanity

To bring out goodness among men

The catalysts guided by the divine

Do live to Improve humanity's lot

They infuse vitality into the wearied

To make the dying come back to life

Such drive the course of renewal

And add value to all that they touch

Except for Prayers (Cont'd)

Thru requests and petitions granted

Men of goodwill and saintly spirits

All live to inject hope for the better

Into the consciousness of humanity

And embody light used by the divine

To counteract the darkness of evil

They hold back tides of wickedness

Unceasing waves that trouble man

And gnaw at the fabric of his soul

Tis evil that'll overwhelm humanity

Except for prayers of saintly souls

That rise to delay judgment's hand

End

Golden Crown of Light

When and where God's truth is loved

With heart, soul, mind and strength

It kindles the awakening of a new life

In divine way of truth, light and love

The believer that continues in the way

Without wavering in his faith or trust

Will mature in spirit to see in purer light

Surely as the morning follows the night

Such will be remade in a divine image

As a giant of faith reborn in new light

Into the realm where God is sovereign

And new man within replaces the old

Golden Crown of Light (Cont'd)

Man can only see in part until rebirth

For he dwells in the place of shadows

In Dalmatia where many are trapped

And hovers between darkness and light

The worthy do escape from Dalmatia

To travel in the power and spirit of God

Beyond limits of horizon to sun's abode

To become reborn as the sons of light

The reborn is a 'sun of righteousness'

For in him life has merged with Light

Such cannot help but speak living truths

That shine true light into hearts of men

End

Kindness and Goodness

The chosen is bestowed with a universal spirit

That enables him to treat all men as kindred

He lives by the golden rule as a righteous soul

Who softens men's stony hearts with kindness

Man that lives for the sake of such goodness

Is well equipped to make resisting souls yield

For he shares in love and speaks truth always

To help reform men 'to vessels useful for God

Kindness yields soberness and introspection

So man can take up his cross and walk with it

Goodness intercedes to avail much happiness

So a man can help another with his burden

Kindness and Goodness (Cont'd)

Humanity wins and no one is left without

When kindness and goodness govern the day

For then is that curse of the earth lifted

That seeds enmity between hope and harvest

End

Sight in Light

Only when man is baptized in the spirit

Can he begin to see in fullness of light

Then is he able to love and give his best

Of his heart, soul, mind and wherewithal

Take the baby awash in mother's womb

Well-fed and at ease in the stream of sap

Receives nourishment that tides him over

But he is in darkness and not able to see

Nutrition in the womb suffices for a time

Helps the baby to develop and to grow

But the ability to 'see' remains lacking yet

For the gift of sight is not activated there

Sight in Light (Cont'd)

Food that sustains in darkness suffices not

When man is born from the womb 'to light

For the world without requires man to see

So he'll know where he fits and role to play

Perception is the 'sight' needed in light

God's gift to help man live victoriously

Tis only for mind and spirit well nourished

For hearts that live in obedience to Truth

Spiritual nourishment affords man the filter

To help purify polluted waters in his mind

Into life's crystal spring to wash the soul

So he is able to perceive in the light of day

End

The Wedge

Trump card of the enemy it turns out to be

To put a wedge 'tween the fathers and sons

A way for him to blight humanity's future

Mock God's creation and set it to naught

Fathers and sons need to be in agreement

So the power of the spirit can flow in full

Father's the generator; son the transformer

But spirit is the power that does the work

The essence of life flows from father to son

The noble is that son who is well-prepared

To be in agreement with the Father's will

In all things and all times as destiny asks

The Wedge (Cont'd)

Wherever father and son are in agreement

There does divine power show forth mightily

To bring about enlightenment and healing

Make for good outcomes in all things in life

But enmity between the son and the father

Is a choke in flow of that which makes good

Takes reconciliation tween fathers and sons

For dearth to be gone so fullness can return

Then is the riches of the divine fully availed

So man can come into rest promised by faith

Into leisure of appointed walks in Providence

Interrupted long ago and faraway in Eden

End

Combatants in the Struggle

The divine Spirit is the essence of life itself

He is the reason for love and therefore life

For man can only come into life thru love

Both with his Creator and with fellowmen

When love of goodness vacates the heart

Man's love for brother will cease to exist

But hatred for fellow man will come to be

To make much room for darkness to thrive

Hatred for brother blinds man's spiritual eye

Robs him of vision to know the good in life

The enemy hates him who sees in true light

And lives in spirit of life and love above all

Combatants in the Struggle (Cont'd)

By willful ignorance and spiritual blindness

The faithless with no love for God within

Unwittingly fights the wrong battles in life

For the cause of darkness to painful regret

It bodes well for humanity for all to know

Everyone is a combatant in a grand struggle

As love fights hatred; light battles darkness

Hope fights despair and life battles death

End

Eye in the Sky

Gift of perception is given to the faithful

In a world full of wolves masked as sheep

To enable him to discern the good from bad

The real from the fake and true from false

Gift of perception brings man much comfort

As protection from wiles and traps around

Works to remove all the fears and doubts

That he may harbor in a world full of caprice

Tis reason for the courage of the faithful

For it affords assurance and peace of mind

Like a monitoring device that reminds man

That he is not alone for God is with him

Eye in the Sky (Cont'd)

Perception is not for the worldly at heart

The lover of materials who fears not God

Tis defensive aide against wicked devices

For man who loves him and fully trusts God

End

Rare and Precious

Gift of perception is truly rare and precious

Tis for the enlightened and receptive in Spirit

All who congregate in the bowel of mercy

And live to watch out for their fellow men

The bowel of mercy is for receiving and sharing

Precious and tender gifts availed by the divine

For the faithful who seeks after righteousness

And helps the cause of life in reversal of death

God's truth condemns not his creation man

Only helps him to see in light of truth and love

But the faithless often refuse needed help

With the illusion that sin is of no consequence

Rare and Precious (Cont'd)

All who dwell in mercy are the bearers of light

To enlighten the dark recesses of men's hearts

So that all can be fed from the bowl of hope

And be renewed by Love's redeeming power

End

In Ever Hopeful Love

The voice of hope can never be silenced

With much good to do and evil to denounce

For light of God shines brightest in the midst

There in darkness where death's spirit lurks

Word of truth that enlightens men's hearts

Declares in hope so the missing can return

Tis the good news that breaks the bad spell

In hearts where evil holds sway over men

Life's word of truth that many men reject

Is never wasted but does the job rather well

Comes home to leave an imprint in the heart

In the soul that the Father has earmarked

In Ever Hopeful Love (Cont'd)

Many are changed with the passage of time

To acknowledge as well as bear true testimony

About redeeming power availed through grace

In ever hopeful love that never gives up hope

End

Hand of Faithfulness

The reborn spirit is the reward and result

With the good and perfect also received

By souls that feed and live in God's truth

Who seek after life's enduring and fulfilling

But sad is the empty soul that rejects truth

For the divine gifts are not availed to him

Discontentment is all that is left in his life

For such who have no reverence for Light

With the right hand man reaches out to God

To receive with humility and thankful joy

But with the left hand he touches the world

To give and share with all in comradeship

Right hand of the faithless withers in time

For without faith man is a stranger to God

Who's not able to receive that which endures

For he lacks the means to reach the divine

Takes right hand to put up resistance to evil

And hold up the shield of faith for protection

In a world full of wickedness and evil deeds

Where acts of men differ from what they say

End

A Sad Tale

The man famished in soul is discontent within

A tale of dearth from spiritual estrangement

He hungers for things that bring no fulfillment

With desires that serve as fuel for raging fires

A malaise that defines many lives on earth

Leads in a downward spiral to the bottomless

To live in unceasing hunger and consumption

As maggots that writhe with insatiable crave

Man trapped in a cycle of wants and purges

Is the fool led away Into the barren lands

'to empty places where there is no living water

With no way of escape save by light of truth

End

A Cross to Carry

Many who profess to seek after divine light

Are only content to keep up appearances

Such are the unfaithful not willing to tarry

To be reborn in spirit into stars of heaven

The true believer has a heavy cross to bear

As a mountain that stands in the way of faith

Though a cup of bitterness repulsive to many

Yet tis the bitter that later turns to the sweet

The way of the cross leads to a strange land

Takes the traveler outside his comfort zone

To vacate position and power in the world

And yet not care for the loss of such props

A Cross to Carry (Cont'd)

What a declaration of faith for all to 'see'

When one man is willing to suffer so much

All in the greater love that counts no hurt

So light can overcome the darkness in many

The journey of faith ends on the distant hill

As the world watches and mocks the noble

But the faithful carries his burden up there

So as to leave the earthy and gain the starry

End

Chiseled in Love

To be rewarded with despise and mockery

And be condemned for the guilt of others

Is the worst that man can do to another

For choosing divine's way of love and hope

Man of good deeds rejected by the world

Through his heavy cross soon does come

Into a place reserved around Divine's table

To experience fullness of the riches of God

The innocent who suffers on love's account

With grace that makes nary a complaint

Soon enters into a covenant with the Divine

To receive the best that Heaven offers man

He's the faithful remade in image of the Creator

One to be well attended by goodness and mercy

For love that proves to be true and unfeigned

And for faith demonstrated beyond all measure

Blessings of the Father do follow him always

The beloved and chosen who dwells secure

Within the cleft hewn in the rock of all ages

With the hammer of faith and chisel of love

End

Common Thread

The faithful is able to see the common thread

The harmony and overall truth in scriptures

That binds the sacred words into one whole

And speaks about a paradise lost to mankind

It resounds with pleas of the Father's anguish

As he waits for the lost children to come home

In pained love that aches with a longing desire

For the creature to bond again with his Creator

It decries the path and pitfalls of transgression

Through prideful disobedience and sinful ways

In sadness for the fruit fallen far from the tree

But with hope always for timely reconciliation

Common Thread (Cont'd)

In words that laud love's long suffering nature

With the readiness to forgive and to forget

Such frame an offer of peace and redemption

So man can know self and find true purpose

In the reconciliation and peace with the father

Man finds that sought and hoped for since Eden

A place of honor reserved and ready welcome

At the Creator's communal feast of love at last

End

Reborn into Immortality

New life awakened by spiritual conception

Is hatched in a cocoon of the Father's love

So man is reborn in the divine image in light

Able to receive the better that's truly sweet

To walk humbly and sincerely before God

In true confession and abstinence from sin

With the divine truths to guide man's steps

Is the all-important decision to make in life

The father does forgive mankind thru love

When the heart is contrite and repentant

Sets such aside for a life of useful service

So redemption's song can ever resound

Some he saves to be woven 'to fabric of life

As sons of light cloaked and duly suited up

With the fleece of the lamb well-sacrificed

That protects mortals from ravages of time

Life is to don immortality's seamless robe

Woven by the timeless hand of the Creator

Tis to have the golden fleece much sought

And walk in the Spirit that vanquishes death

Robes are for his tabernacles among men

The beloved chosen to be dwelling places

Such baptized in truth and fire of the Spirit

Are suited to join Life's everlasting throng

End

Strong Faith

To be ageless and timeless are for the immortals

Those judged worthy of eternity with the father

Such were once debased but due to be exalted

To be accepted and woven into the fabric of life

Faith does persevere to do the amazing in life

In the long suffering kindness that forgives much

To turn tiny seeds into mighty oaks of the forest

And mere mortals 'to giants in touch with heaven

The seed nourished by truth takes time to mature

Into strong faith able to call life back from death

Tis for those able to suffer for the cause of Love

Who bear well the heavy cross that leads to Life

It exacts a heavy toll to bear good fruit in light

But great vision and strong faith comes by such

Tis a given for those recreated in Father's image

For men reborn in light through redeeming love

Through the process of suffering for goodness

Man is changed from base into a heavenly star

In glory of the new found through the cross

That outweighs the pain and death of the old

End

Deep Nail Marks

All who have borne faith's cross up the hill

Know the pain that sacrificial love exacts

In passion shared thru common experience

By all who long for goodness of the divine

The crucified are bearers of the nail marks

Whose lives are laid down for love of Truth

With deep wounds inflicted by the hateful

As badge of honor and crest of the divine

Takes the deep nails to keep the old buried

And same it takes to set man free into Life

For there's a special place reserved for such

Where crucifixion's nails have made marks

Deep Nail Marks (Cont'd)

The deep nails used to crucify the faithful

Are painful yet soothed by mercy's touch

Takes such pain to open up a wellspring

And make pure water of life to flow freely

In pain one suffers for many to be healed

As acceptable sacrifice deep in man's soul

To embrace such is to receive of life freely

So goodness and mercy can ever abound

End

Place of New Name

Goodness and mercy are always in good attendance

As currency exchanged for the treasures of heaven

For the man whose heart beats in compassionate love

Who travels on the lighted path of the noble in spirit

Tis unnecessary to rush about but to travel calmly on

In the amazing place where man receives in mercy

For therein the good and perfect soothe ever gently

In the place where sins and trespasses are no more

The place of new life is for all who've been adopted

As sons of light and bestowed with heavenly gifts

In a Spirit that makes the hidden to become plain

And enables man to walk with wisdom in command

Place of New Name (Cont'd)

Tis an essence that wills and acts through the faithful

To bring about fulfilling and enduring outcomes in life

By new names and in handiworks that abound in light

As branches of the tree of life to produce the worthy

End

Power of the Anointing

The faithful man that has the Father's investiture

Knows the way and is called to point it out to others

He's the elder brother who must teach the younger

And be the guide for those seeking but yet to find

He's to bring nothing in the call save a loving heart

For he will have access to all needed thru Providence

All by the divine anointing that makes much possible

So his wishes are granted and petitions met as due

Man bestowed with the anointing is an exalted one

Who has nothing but yet has everything that he needs

Knows not all but has knowledge of the prescient

By power that serves true faithfulness with due glory

Power of the Anointing (Cont'd)

All's done and shared in grace when the olive blooms

So that many can have the blessings that peace avails

Creator reserves much for the anointed who shares

And resupplies him with what is needed in the way

End

The Citizen

From the darkness of the world into marvelous light

The old joins in spirit with the divine to produce a hybrid

Such is a higher breed that's streamlined and quickened

A creature reborn in spirit that is able to soar freely

Weighty things of the world are pruned from the reborn

With the needful left to replace the fluffy and wasteful

So man's spirit can be free to ascend to exalted realms

To converse in places where eternal spirits congregate

Through wisdom's veil to reach the light and starry

Is for man at peace who has reconciled with the Father

To become a citizen of that certain city of Jerusalem

With ability to read the writings that spell divine edicts

The Citizen (Cont'd)

Such must ask of the father all that his heart desires

And be ever willing to do what the Creator asks of him

He need only buckle down for the never ending ride

In faith's carousel that turns tween heaven and earth

End

Truth in Pictures

The divine mind expressed through mortals

Is mystery and genius of words of scripture

Mostly figurative but yet true and fulfilling

With nary a word that is out of place or time

The fruit of the fig from the tree of life

Is for those with good and certain measure

Men full of understanding and true wisdom

Who are ever in communion with the Divine

Man's languages do discriminate and divide

To muddle communication among humanity

Tis borne of Babel to throw man for a loop

So that the earthen is not taken to heaven

Truth in Pictures (Cont'd)

The heavenly conversations unfold as images

In the light of truth that needs no translation

Tis true a picture is worth a thousand words

In medium that is universal and tells no lies

End

Family Portrait

From the heavenly heights the faithful can see

A true picture of the world with eye of the spirit

For no longer will such be deceived by the world

When man is able to see from the mountain top

The true oracle speaks as the divine commands

As God's tabernacle through whom truth spills

To communicate in words that paint pictures

And to declare in love as Heaven duly informs

The language of pictures is of light and truth

Impressions in time and place that tell no lies

Effective and pure medium to teach the mind

Cleanse humanity's soul and nourish the spirit

Family Portrait (Cont'd)

Words of scripture do join to paint a portrait

To frame one grand picture of the family of God

Speaks about choices, actions and outcomes

For those willing to embrace the true and pure

A quickening in mind with a spiritual eye to see

One's self and place within the fold of humanity

Is fulfillment availed as new is reborn from old

Through obedience and trust in God's promises

End

Restored to Glory

Restoration is evoked from the hub of creation

As divine's heart desires and womb of life gives

From thence issues forth the power to rebuild

To bring the dying and broken down back to life

Takes restoration to put content into the empty

Tis means by which the moribund is re-vitalized

And better things are brought out from the old

Such as availed for the certain and orderly man

Restoration will not commence duly in man's life

Until by faith he's immersed and baptized in truth

Then will his walk be simple and orderly in light

Immune from the uncertainty that leads astray

Restored to Glory (Cont'd)

Certainty makes for simplicity and orderliness

But variance compounds life with disorderliness

Tis not the heavenly way to bless confusion

Or the way of glory to restore the uncertain

End

Seeds within the Mountain

The mountainous often appears unexpectedly

To forestall the commencement of restoration

Takes wisdom and power availed through faith

To pass through that which stands in man's way

There's delightful discovery within the mountain

Seeds of the new that God uses to glorify man

Much like golden flakes borne of a pure stream

Deep within that which seems insurmountable

Much is laden in that which stands in the way

For the mountain is there to shield the precious

Seeds touched by the divine that are found within

As treasures well-hidden for the beloved to have

Seeds within the Mountain (Cont'd)

Such are seeds of glory that spring to life in light

In full display so that heaven and earth can attest

What Creation has in store for the faithful man

When the mountain dreaded breaks out in song

End

Love Reconnected

Man's desire to reconnect with the divine

May cost the faithful his place in the world

Turns out to be a worthy sacrifice after all

In order to find welcome into realm of light

Confident glow surrounds the reconnected

Governs everything that he says and does

Tis the light of hope that attracts all seekers

Gift to be used in noble service of the Father

The heart lit aflame with power of the divine

No longer makes room for the spirit of fear

Has an assurance borne of love reconnected

As the testament of life and reason for hope

Love Reconnected (Cont'd)

Spirit of power and sharp mind equips man

To know the necessary and the good to do

Always with due and prescient knowledge

So things fit well when love is reconnected

Face of the future is when all's done in love

As the time to redress and not to impress

To treasure the enduring and fulfilling always

In meekness that inherits the earth for good

End

The Trailblazers

A critical mass of men and women there is

All over the world that love the way of light

Such have walked in faithfulness and truth

To arrive at the place close to divine's heart

Men bestowed with the heavenly attributes

Thru an unending and everlasting dynamic

Are enlightened ones held in the divine palm

As one carefully holds the precious pearl

The stars of the night sky are their emblems

Gardeners that tend earthly lots with care

Each star occupies the plot ordained for it

Foreknown and predestinated from time

The Trailblazers (Cont'd)

Each is a trail-blazer to break new grounds

The starry used to show and lead the way

As vehicles to realize the new from the old

So divine light can have full sway of day

End

Age of the Perfected

All of creation waits for those bred in the bowel of mercy

Who have been well prepared to make things right again

With foresight from experiences borne in love's cocoon

To reflect the pattern for victorious living in the new age

The visionaries and luminaries to guide men 'to the future

Are afforded the knowledge and wisdom that is needed

And do already live today in the mind-set of tomorrow

With principles and guidelines needed to master the new

There's silence ordained at the turning point of this age

So man can stop and reconsider the errors of his past

Then will things turn to point upwards and heavenward

To usher in the dawn of the glorious day of a new man

Age of the Perfected (Cont'd)

The golden age of the pure in heart and noble in spirit

Is season for those who have chosen to live in true light

Immortal souls who've been grafted 'to the tree of life

Who've chosen wisdom of the eternal over the worldly

Then is no reason for man to exhaust precious time

To seek after unfulfilling and dispiriting things in life

Or search for a futile balance between good and evil

When he is freed from darkness to attain the perfect

End

Redeemable in Man

The noble and faithful souls have been destined

As the seedlings for life in the new advent age

And the depositories of the spark that brings on

An awakening and a quickening in the lifeless

Tis the emergence of the 'suns' of righteousness

To usher in the spirit of regeneration in new life

And thaw the frozen in humanity's wintry soul

So mankind can rise in a new spring of hope

The flesh is needed for man's brief time on earth

But it is the culprit and the inhibitor of his spirit

Such that leads man to an unceasing war within

To make him susceptible to defeats and stumbles

Redeemable in Man (Cont'd)

Man's ego is culprit and Achilles heel in this war

For tis a chink in the armor of his spiritual defense

Only a misconceived notion of his self-importance

That is an unruly ghost given to offend the Spirit

Man's flesh matters little in life's overall scheme

His flesh is briefly here and soon crumbles away

But his spirit is the only redeemable entity in him

If he can be awaked and transformed to new life

End

Glory of the Cross

There's a seed of the divine buried within each man

Tis a spirit of goodness that waits and hopes in him

Becomes precious and of great value in due time

If the dirt of the ego is dislodged and washed away

Tis the reason for the dreaded passion and agony

For instituting the process symbolized by the cross

It's shame and humiliation are the perfect tools

To nail down man's flesh and bury the ego in dust

The cross is bold declaration for ascension of spirit

An icon of crucifixion that serves as best platform

For man to observe and learn clearly for all time

The mystery of spiritual purification thru humility

Glory of the Cross (Cont'd)

To understand the glory that the cross spawns

Is to marvel at the unfathomable wisdom of God

The ego denied of the praise it seeks soon vanishes

Into the nothingness of dust from which it came

The cross is an emblem of man's flesh rid of ego

Poised for takeoff to join the ranks of immortals

Tis there with his flesh yielded totally to the divine

That man is fitted with wings of an exalted spirit

It changes shameful death into a glorious victory

To afford the man without ego a new lease on life

So he can realize all that God has ordained for him

Who risked all that flesh can give in search of Life

End

New Life Awaits

New Life in light is ordained for him

Who hears, obeys and shares in truth

In place reserved for such that trust

Who live and walk in the divine spirit

All in holiness for the hearts that heed

For the reborn that live in the new life

With Ghost to teach and Spirit to lead

As divine's dwelling places on earth

To desire, to ask and receive in love

Is ultimate gift from Father to sons

As precious key that opens the vault

So that sons are well set in the future

New Life Awaits (Cont'd)

Life looks not to the past but future

There to produce much worthy fruits

For only the dead abound in the past

As pillars of salt that litter the land

The past makes for a shadowy veil

A cloak of darkness that hinders life

For Creator fulfills his promises in light

For all awakened by the call of Love

End

In Regenerative Splendor

To pretend to be in spiritual fellowship

By false confessions and manipulations

Is the suit of wolves in sheep's clothing

Who aim to set the divine will at naught

The unworthy partakers of divine grace

Infect charity's feast as unjustified flies

And exploit love's communion of light

In misguided deeds thru unbridled lust

The faithful who's been worthy of grace

Is not to be yoked with him who is not

So he can be led into the greater light

Availed only to 'good' and noble souls

The good in creation are drawn together

To seek with great vision and strong faith

In a place where time, order and purpose

Blend together in regenerative splendor

End

Language of the Heart

All who are woven into the fabric of Life

Are tuned in spirit to hear the inaudible

In language of hearts that is clearly heard

When the flesh yields for spirit to govern

Then all do speak and all can understand

The father, sons and every true believer

Such purified of heart and noble in spirit

Who live in time to serve the divine will

The hearts joined in love's grand labor

Tend a garden where goodness abounds

Wherein all beat together in light of truth

To produce a delightful harvest in time

Language of the Heart (Cont'd)

The heart desires so the eye can behold

When all is hoped thru the power of God

No longer need for man to will and to run

When his spirit is at ease in Life's long ride

Lane to victory in life is open for the heart

That has found comfort within the divine

He hurries not and so wastes not much

When man's on board and settled in Love

End

Wellspring of Life

The fruit copies well the tree

That is commended into Life

For righteousness of the tree

Does show forth in the fruit

It bodes well for the faithful

Who attend to heed as well

To the man that dwells within

And always speaks in truth

From the wellspring of life

To give voice to the eternal

For all who will listen in time

To note while there is hope

Wellspring of Life (Cont'd)

He is one well-tuned as due

To divine's frequency of love

From whence man is availed

Truths otherwise well-hidden

Holy Ghost is he who brings

Prescient knowledge to light

Source of the true and pure

Conduit to God for only a few

The faithful do tarry in hope

And wait for Him who knows

For victory is only for those

Informed in love from above

End

Of Healing and Restoration

Healing and restoration are gifts

Bestowed by divine intervention

When man has done all he can

To find answers but to no avail

Healing is the swipe of the sword

That cuts thru life's tangled knot

An answer for that unique issue

That's been bedeviling for awhile

Healing smoothens the thorny

That holds up increase for man

Fixes the broken to make it go

But good to go makes not anew

Of Healing and Restoration (Cont'd)

Restoration takes place over time

In dawn of regeneration season

Takes same to revitalize the dead

And make the new out of the old

Restoration is kin with wholeness

Tis comprehensive and covers all

A new and fresh start from God

That's only for the reborn in light

Restoration is the best reserved

Heaven's priceless gift of the new

That springs from womb of Life

Under the aegis of divine's mercy

End

Food for the Sublime

Tis the desire of the righteous

That makes for things sublime

For man is such as he feeds

In foolishness or in wisdom

Within the figures of speech

That frame nuggets of truth

Are polishing hands of Love

To make the obedient shine

The veil of true understanding

Is lifted by the divine hand

Through faith's abiding love

For all who are willing to trust

Food for the Sublime (Cont'd)

To receive in love from God

And abound in divine mercy

The sincere and humble know

To ask in faith that's strong

The precious gifts are pearls

Though not for the swine

Not for those that profane

And deem grace for naught

The gift that comforts man

Is Holy Ghost from above

A priceless gift that comes

Only by long suffering hope

End

Golden Flakes of Mercy

Mercy drops come down freely from above

As showers of latter rain to fill up the empty

Tis sweetness duly come in the season of hope

In fulfillment of love that is best saved for last

Gifts received in mercy are not to be wasted

Such are not for all but for the chosen faithful

For all who labor in love and in righteous works

Who are well watched with pride from above

From behind the veil mercy begins her journey

As golden flakes that descend to alight in love

On the righteous as divine showers that delight

For the heart that can see HIM hidden by light

Golden Flakes of Mercy (Cont'd)

As spirit takes flight while raptured in prayer

The hand of Providence shows in timely order

And delightful moments come to uplift the soul

In such sweetness borne of mercy from above

End

Spirit of Uncertainty

The unclean do fester in earthly affairs
And manifests as the spirit of uncertainty
That propels mankind all over the place
In hurried frenzies of restless activities

Man not at rest in spirit is neither in flesh
And is afforded little peace or fulfillment
Such is very hard-pressed to do the right
But easily given to do the wrong instead

Many seek solace in company of the lost
And join herds that are headed for death
Such prefer to be part of the in-crowd
Instead of a new life alone if need be

Spirit of Uncertainty (Cont'd)

The uncertain is aimless and rudderless

And casts about in listless convulsions

With unnecessary fits of fear and doubt

In sundry illusions that bubble and bust

End

The Insatiable

Uncertainty brings man an empty feeling

And a wishful craving for something else

Makes him wish to be and have another

Instead of what he is and what he has

The uncertain will make accommodation

For mistruths and compromises in his life

He's such that is given to finger-pointing

And loves to shift the blames on to others

Uncertainty is borne of an earthen spirit

That breeds jealousy and discontentment

It tortures man's soul in unceasing desires

In wanton and unfulfilling consumptions

The Insatiable (Cont'd)

Tis such restlessness and dissatisfaction

That hinder from making a commitment

As good intentions do turn out for worse

In mood swings that change as the wind

The uncertain is prone to reject the truth

Which he knows in his soul to be true

Yet his heart is troubled with much angst

Conflicted with guilt for refusing the light

End

Man of Good Faith

Truth affords man a mind-set

To see all things in a new light

Helps him to fjord the Jordan

Into the place of good promise

The heart that's washed in truth

Has to come about first in life

Before purification of the spirit

And divine anointing can follow

All such that Love has promised

If kept on desktop of the heart

Do remind about due judgment

And the way of escape for man

Man of Good Faith (Cont'd)

Takes an honest search of soul

To put focus on the important

And bring the needful to mind

So the trivial counts for less

Good faith it takes to choose

The eternal over the passing

The starry 'stead of the earthly

And Life over death as ought

End

Child to Man

In time the faithful child of grace

Will have his life resorted as due

To become the man duly anointed

Who stands tall under divine mercy

The man of mercy does well to live

By a higher standard pure and true

As a flag bearer for truth and light

Ever in the spirit of forgiving love

He's one that is sanctified in truth

Such that wisdom crowns with life

Shielded from that which corrupts

And mars the unsuspecting with evil

Child to Man (Cont'd)

He's one remade in a divine image

And called to forgive all in mercy

Always with best in mind for man

In wisdom that is reflected in love

Such gets to wear eternity's cloak

And can travel anywhere in spirit

As trustee of seeds for the new

Who comes in a season of change

End

Embodiment of Truth

The noble in spirit is universal

Not bound by space and time

Can travel to far-away places

To realms beyond man's flesh

Faith makes an accommodation

For the truth alive in the heart

That springs forth to life as due

When destiny's moment arrives

He never wanders far from truth

When man is anchored on faith

With good and certain purpose

In thoughts, words and actions

Embodiment of Truth (Cont'd)

As seasons and time converge

The words become the faithful

And man becomes the words

As a living embodiment of truth

End

Branch of the Tree

Alas the hands of humble adoration

Have merged with wings of mercy

As the faithful is set free by truth

To soar into the realm of the eagle

Faithless that wanders from truth

Wings to bear him up will be clipped

He'll not rise with freedom's wind

But only know the dust of the lowly

He's salt that has lost its true savor

No longer good for anything in life

Not in God's way or in the world's

But only good as dirt of the earth

The soul well washed in living truth

Belongs with man reborn in light

Thru the certainty borne of eternity

As spirit readied for works of glory

The one anointed in the divine vein

Is issued the passport of eternal life

Into a realm of the pure and true

As a branch of the righteous tree

Man's lot is with God and not men

To receive life's good and perfect

In requests and petitions granted

For the branch that withstands evil

End

Uncertain Bearings

He's a man of uncertain bearings

Who's never able to find true self

Always at the wrong place is he

To do things when he should not

The uncertain lives to be praised

In passing thrills of the moment

With neither fear nor reverence

For precious things from above

The emptiness of unrealized goals

And sourness of unfulfilled dreams

Is for the man that lives by sight

Who walks not in wisdom's light

Uncertain Bearings (Cont'd)

The fruitless becomes his harvest

As uncertainty rules man's heart

A veil of blindness covers the eye

And a dimness pervades the soul

The blind follower after the world

Soon wades into a dismal flood

To be deluged and carried along

Into a wasteland of hopelessness

End

Lamp for Others

The true and real can be found by all

Through the vision inspired by love

The faithful that has come into light

Must guide and lead others therein

The faithful is the lamp for the blind

The many who are lost in the way

Such will find the way soon enough

When there is a guide near to help

Essence of goodness is compromised

In haste, short-cuts and quick routes

For great havoc is wreaked on those

Who fall prey to ill-conceived notions

Lamp for Others (Cont'd)

Subservience to the corrupting spirit

Will lead men to profane the sacred

To cause a cessation of fortune's tide

And make the blissful difficult to find

Many men can no longer tell apart

The acceptable from what's disdained

As the spirit of the world prevails

To cause sin and death to abound

Divine wisdom counsels all to know

That the man freed by light of truth

Has a divine mandate and also power

To free all souls still bound in darkness

End

The Entombed

The cleansing water of the living truths

That washes the heart of the faithful

Turns into joyful wine of marital bliss

As man's spirit joins up with the divine

Such that is joined dwells not in tombs

But has entered 'to eternity's freedom

Where much is availed to him as due

Far from the dead end of faithlessness

The future is veiled for tomb dwellers

As to look back is all that's left for such

Thoughts on things that might've been

About a past that should be forgotten

The Entombed (Cont'd)

Without vision man sacrifices his future

To become a blind follower of crowds

Who lacks the anointing and immunity

Availed by justification through godliness

End

Scourge of Lust and Greed

Creatures that presume to be the Creator

Make themselves to be arbiters of truth

And are given to choose might over right

Through manipulative schemes and plots

Many lust after sweet meats of the world

With no regard and reverence for deity

Such devour with little regard for others

In obsessed pursuit of the soft and dainty

Man that sees cup of life as running empty

Rushes about to have it when he wants it

Such care not about the welfare of others

And do scuttle humanity's vessels of hope

Scourge of Lust and Greed (Cont'd)

Many who squeeze life out of situations

Muddle thru life devoid of wholeness

Such hoard and choke under possessions

With little fear for the judgment of light

Hogs live under lust's deluge and delusion

Smitten with the blindness of fool's gold

Too quick and too soon without regard

For the common wealth of humankind

Unceasing clamor and lust for the fake

Leaves man's milk of understanding dry

To make room for wickedness to flourish

And give evil ground to come to fullness

Scourge of lust and Greed (Cont'd)

The prince of darkness is now entrenched

In minds and places where he ought not be

So that the hand of justice is now raised

As upheavals for due changes now visit man

End

Soul of the Divine

The spirit freed soon receives

A sweet cup due the righteous

That overflows with the good

In mercies tender and divine

Such does live with good hope

And is able to bring new life

Into situations bereft of hope

From a heavenly side of earth

He labors not for love of self

But for God and fellow man

Possessions and earthly glory

Not for him with soul divine

Soul of the Divine (Cont'd)

He blazes a new trail for all

In sights and hope rekindled

As lost things are found again

And dead things are revitalized

Spirit remade by divine design

Is one counted with the noble

In a starry vein and anointing

To find delight in realm of light

End

Womb of the Immaculate

The spirits of the just are in perfection

In truth, light and love on to eternity

Such are joined to the universal mind

And led to welcome in divine's abode

The web of life of the noble-hearted

Is a living network akin to a beehive

Where all thoughts blend together

In goodwill to find a common cause

Goodness is served with due purpose

All in blissful moments and in peace

From the exhaustion of the earthly

Into the revitalizing of the heavenly

Womb of the Immaculate (Cont'd)

To obey and serve the divine call

Through foot-steps guided in light

Is to live for glory of the honorable

And goodness that endures in time

Earthly stripes avail heavenly glory

As the glittering crown of Wisdom

To the man purified in light of truth

Is the immaculate borne in time

End

Beware of the Storm

In soul that has been purified in truth

Waits the heart that'll be God's temple

Tis the prize that should be desired

And hoped for by all true believers

The life sought after by the faithful

In way that perfects the spirit within

Is not for commercial exploitation

Or for the profane after vain glory

The great trap of fame and fortune

Which many are unable to overcome

In hearts where those rule the day

Will prince of darkness come to stay

Beware of the Storm (Cont'd)

Therein the restorative divine stream

Begins to dry up and is soon replaced

By the raging storm of Rehab's fury

For therein is the divine prostituted

Lust for earthly possessions corrupts

And ties up the soul of humankind

Blessings possess not but gently alight

On the hearts that are God's temples

End

Teach the Young Better

The noises and twinkling lights of this world

Make for a formidable obstacle for the unwary

Tis a precipitous slope and daunting challenge

From which the young are to be weaned away

There's burping and throwing up in faith's way

But longsuffering love and due patience it takes

For the matured in faith to feed well the young

As the milk of the word is rejected at first taste

Fate and fortune of mankind lies with the young

Leaves the elder in faith with much work to do

For the enemy has schemes to lure such minds

With manipulative traps and deceitful promises

Teach the Young (Cont'd)

The young is attracted to the seemingly easy

Often chooses to cut corners and bend rules

Unbeknown to the young who does not know

There is no quick and easy way up victory hill

Tis a long and arduous climb to the summit

To grand stand where blessings are ordained

The faithful must be patient and full of hope

As he deals with the young who are the future

End

Harbinger of the Greater

Many come to an arrested development

By indolence thru partial understanding

As flawed teachings bedevil humankind

To make the promising wither in the way

For sojourner thru night's dark passage

The lesser enlightenment will not suffice

Tis in the vision yielded by greater light

That life's victory is soon availed to man

The faithful that has been established

Through the journey of faith unto mercy

Must return to find those still enamored

With the watered of the sweet and easy

Harbinger of the Greater (Cont'd)

As great spiritual famine besets the land

Lesser enlightenment rules men's minds

In partial knowledge and understanding

That forestalls a break of dawn in hearts

But some are harbingers of greater light

Well prepared to bring true illumination

To all who seek to escape the shadows

And help usher them into a fuller vision

All who've been to the abode of clouds

Are to help clear up the choked streams

Filled up with the debris of misguidance

And bring living water to the thirsty souls

End

Drunk with Milk

Misguidance will rear the promising

Into retardation and un-fulfillment

A spiritual dwarf who soon becomes

Blind to the true and real riches of life

The child that should have been a man

Soon settles in life as a man-child stuck

Lame and ill-equipped to finish the race

Due to the lack of better understanding

Unable to make it to the mountaintop

He'll never come into true knowledge

For he is precluded to see in full light

With no exposure to the greater truth

Drunk with milk (Cont'd)

He's a milk drinker drunk with the easy

Who cannot eat the meat of the word

That affords man strength and wisdom

To undergo full transformation in spirit

End

True Cathedrals

He who has scaled the mountain

Faces opposition and contention

From those stuck below in grace

The vain who exploit truth for gain

Such are like clouds without rain

Limited with partial understanding

Who budge not from misguidance

With obsession for feast of grace

Such are the masters who package

Religion as commercial enterprises

Whose hearts are after the worldly

As seekers after fame and fortune

True Cathedrals (Cont'd)

Men who excel at marketing religion

With lofty schemes and sales charts

And build imposing cathedrals to suit

As shrines to the self in name of God

But God cares not for such Cathedrals

Only for the hearts and souls purified

In the light of truth and stream of love

For such are places where HE dwells

End

Trap of the Enemy

The purified heart is a 'Catherine'

Such ones in non-descript places

Used as true Cathedrals to model

And help restore lost souls of men

The masters of religion of this age

Haunted by shadows and eclipses

Build kingdoms of men on earth

In their gilded churches of stones

With words that enthrall and charm

In promises of hope and salvation

That which only God avails to man

Some now claim to be able to give

Trap of the Enemy (Cont'd)

There men have gone back to Babel

In attempts to take earth to heaven

But tis heaven to earth thru the light

So it can be here below as up above

Lust for material is an insidious trap

In love feigned for God just for gain

Enemy uses this ploy to much effect

To blunt the message of love and life

End

Keeper of the Watch

There's a voiceless means to communicate
That the fully matured in spirit is tuned to
The rare and precious gift of the Holy Ghost
Used to make all the needful things known

The ability to live in harmony with nature
Is the ultimate desire of the Divine for man
For shepherds to care for the sheep in love
And gardeners to tend garden-earth well

A good shepherd is that householder fit
Whose treasure is new come out of the old
He's the faithful that abides in secret place
For he lives in the kingdom that a few know

New that emerges from carcass of the old

Is the seedling and staple of the new age

Householder fit is regenerator and rebuilder

God's gift to willing mankind for restoration

Such speak about things that conform not

To mainstream thinking and popular beliefs

As sounder of alarms who save the attentive

And keep dutiful watch in man's night time

End

Brother's Keepers

Christ is 'compassion' by one for another

Man that has same honors God's wishes

For each man that is his brother's keeper

Obeys a command very dear to the Divine

The faithful that learns and loves to keep

Good company with fellow man in love

Soon comes to walk in divine company

And be counted among Heaven's chosen

Good company is like the Samaritan kept

With the man robbed and left as nothing

Not in false companionship like Caan did

So life is rescued from the jaws of death

Brother's Keepers (Cont'd)

Life is reserved for the compassionate

Who truly love and live by the golden rule

In an exalted place that most know not

For many compromise love's trusting link

End

Breaking the Chains

There is the man recreated in divine image

When spirit mounts up with wings of eagle

With a heart that beats with compassion

And a mind re-connected with the Creator

An ordained and purposed life awaits him

Whose soul is washed and purified in truth

A place in congregation of the living is his

As one deemed worthy to serve the divine

Man has to stand tall so as to be counted

With the gift that mercy affords in light

He's to overcome fears and venture afar

To where those perfected in love attend

Breaking the Chains (Cont'd)

Man appointed to step outside the box

And break the chain of human mediocrity

Must go beyond the gates of the known

For thereabouts is glory ordained for him

End

Banded Together

All who are reborn in light are banded in spirit

By the love and desire to please the Creator

Tis not fame and fortune that motivates such

That labor not for vain glory or man's praise

The hearts joined together beat in true love

In service to each other with loftiness of spirit

Such are drawn to place close to God's heart

To be covered with ointment of his anointing

Hearts close to each other will beat together

And sing in a tune of universal brotherhood

To recommend the virtues of the golden rule

And evoke a spirit of love's refreshing breeze

Banded Together (Cont'd)

The spirit that is so elusive in the world today

Love of brother and togetherness of purpose

Is found to echo the heartbeat of the heaven

In hearts that beat together and sing in love

Hearts that communicate with each other

Will send and receive messages as needed

In a realm where there are new songs to sing

In vibrations of love between God and man

End

Truth Speaks for Self

The enlightened inner man can never be mistaken

The wrapping may change and the shade may vary

But the content of the package remains the same

For all are same when wrought from mold of mercy

Message of truth is undeniable and speaks for itself

For the voice of compassion can never be mistaken

Tis a voice recognition that's effected thru the divine

So the sheep can always know the shepherd's voice

The voice of love and truth is always identifiable

Same shows up in all colors, tongues and cultures

The believer who truly loves can perceive the divine

Regardless of whatever guise or form he appears in

End

Earthly stripes avail heavenly glory

As the glittering crown of Wisdom

To the man purified in light of truth

Is the glorious availed in due time

OTHER BOOKS BY KALU ONWUKA INCLUDE-

(Poetry)

Anthems in the Glorious Dawn

In Enchantment of Eternity

A Splendid Awakening

The Melody of Light

(Books for Spirit, Mind and Body)

Nuggets of Resurrection

Pulses of the Divine Heart

Etching for the Faithful Heart

No Hurry to Horeb

(Quotations and Insights)

Capsules of Divine Splendor

All titles are available as paperbacks or e-books and may be purchased through many retail outlets/distribution channels. All titles may also be purchased through Granada Publishers at **granadapublishing.com.** In addition, excerpts of the author's works can be read through his website at **kaluonwuka.com.**

Kalu Onwuka is a prolific author who writes about faith walk in this new age of man's spiritual awareness. He offers tit-bits on how to find a balance between the heavenly and earthly through his writings. He is a man of many accomplishments and draws inspirational insights from experiences in many areas of life. He is a *Teacher, Poet, Lyricist, Essayist, Engineer and Entrepreneur.* He is married, a father of five and lives in Southern California.

He is the author of the *On the Golden Strand* series which are discourses that encapsulate his spiritual experiences on the walk of faith. These include The *Nuggets of Resurrection, Pulses of the Divine Heart, Etching for the Faithful Heart and No Hurry to Horeb.* He is also the author of the *Poems in Faithfulness to the Divine* Series which are books of poetry and songs. These include *Anthems in the Glorious Dawn, In Enchantment of Eternity, Tones of the Stellar, A Splendid Awakening, Melody of Light, Capsules of Divine Splendor* and other books.

www.ingramcontent.com/pod-product-compliance
Lightning Source LLC
Chambersburg PA
CBHW070350070426
42446CB00050BA/2793